Sappho, I Should have Listened
and other poems

Sappho, I Should have Listened
and other poems

Ellen Tsagaris

Ellen M. Tsagaris

918*studio*
LeClaire, Iowa

Sappho, I Should have Listened
and other poems

Ellen Tsagaris

52 pages
published by 918*studio*
isbn 0-615454208
isbn-13 978-0-615-45420-7

copyright © 2011 Ellen Tsagaris
printed in the United States of America
all rights reserved

cover design and typography by Rivertown Creative

For Mamma

POEMS

River Lines	1
Fishwife Barbie	3
When I heard the Learned Professor's Wife	7
In this Your Home so Quiet	8
Loving you has exhausted me	9
The Vampyre Doll Collector	10
Ballet Entrenous	14
For Anne Rice	16
Vampyre	18
The Blood Countess	19
Doppelgänger	22
Lucifer; if You could be Forgiven	24
Chippiannock Sanctuary	25
A Child's Winter	28
Hymn to Arachne	29
Allensworth, CA	30
On Poe's Bicentennial	31
Dickinson meets Hemingway	33
Witch Etiquette	34
Anne and Sylvia	36
Hanged Woman	37
Sappho, I Should have Listened	38
Acknowledgements	40

RIVER LINES

Once I lived near the shores of an ocean.
I stood and gazed at its infinity,
I wondered at its vastness,
I thrilled at its beauty,
And I longed for my river.

My heart cried out for the roaring rapids,
My hands wanted to sequester and caress the small, smooth stones.
The white beach was pretty, but the gritty river sand
Was what made up my chemistry.
Atlantic, Pacific, Aegean, and Mediterranean
Are Pretty names,
But Mississippi is a far mightier title,
It has substance and
Old Mis has been the fluid highway
Of my life's journey.

He is the road that leads out,
And the path that brings me home, time and
Time again.
All I love are buried on its shores,
I waded my youth in its shoals,
Looking at its tiniest creatures under a
Microscope in field biology,
Thrilling at its larger denizens as I watched them
Jump amid the muddy waves from the safety rail of the bridge.

The oceans are wide, deep, and pretty.
They murmur their stories and their Sirens lure,
But the River is my family, and for
Love of its swampy shores, and
Lonely islands, and Ferry Tales,
I came Home.

FISHWIFE BARBIE

How she caterwauls
Down the street,
Bottle blonde hair
Gray at the roots
Middle age sag and
Unflattering pulls of gravity in
Bad places ...

She lives for color in her world,
Blues, and reds, and oh those
Pretty little purples,
Mother's helpers all.

All because she has to wear the pants.
Being a prof's wife is hard, all those
Dusty books, but she discouraged that right away

And the private school, her children
Would be the light of the morning star
Talentless and whey faced,
Automatons who stagger through
Life, their batteries not working right..

All but her Ella, her Lolita
On a skateboard, and
OH, what was that man
Doing, reading again!!

Books were ok, if she could
Swing back a Zima and
Get a dime bag from the
Paperback bookstore

All that romance, and so short—
Big books were such a waste, and
Too many words!!

No one understood her—
People were so friendly before,
Her little town brain
Fairly popped with fresh
Gossip, each
Kernel as tasty as any

Redenbacher.

But now,
Everyone ran in when they saw her,
The prof's hearing was going, too,
HE didn't seem to realize she was talking to
HIM.

And the young babysitters
That showed up at her door
Sneered at her behind her back.

Oh, she heard them alright,
She saw them through the bottom of the
Zima bottle, smiling at Prof,
Glancing sideways.

The last baby had been too much;
Potty training sent her to mixing
Mountain Dew with Gin,
To talking way too loud,
To forget how to pronounce, "TEN-Yore."

She could remember it wasn't
"Ten-fore," and she knew
People laughed at her.

She missed the cows
At her farm in Michigan.
Too bad they'd had to leave,
Too bad her daddy's lecherous
Eye had settled on her—

Too bad the nice folks at the foster home
Couldn't have kept her . .

SAPPHO, I SHOULD HAVE LISTENED

Ah, well, she wasn't going to take
It.

She'd show Prof and all of them.

But Prof still didn't hear her.
She had to screech, and the vein
Stood out in her neck, and her pale,
Pasty skin blotched red,
And her bottle blonde hair got frizzy,
Her yard sale Laura Ashley
Finery grew tight and sad and
Threadbare.

And there were no more
Cocktail parties and
Midnight dinners at Old Citadel.
And her caterwauling fishwifery
Turned to desperate housewifery.

WHEN I HEARD THE LEARNED PROFESSOR'S WIFE

When I heard the Learned Professor's Wife
Spout her philosophy, I heard the theme from
"Coal Miner's Daughter in my head."
When I saw her beady eyes pop like
Tiny beetles cooking and exploding
On campfire spaghetti cooked on an
Open flame,
When I saw and felt her wizened little hands
Pound a mad tempo on the hood of my car,
When I smelled the sick perfume of
Envy, misery, and desperation on her breath
Along with cheap gin,
I felt uncommonly sad.
When I thought of her learned husband, spouting philosophy,
To students he would fail passionately if they did not paint the scarred
Wooden paneling on his crooked house,
I heard the theme from Looney Tunes,
And looked up at the heavens, to see a small,
Peroxide blonde hair drift down to their unkempt yard
And was glad mine was not the life of the Learned Professor's
Wife.

IN THIS YOUR HOME SO QUIET

In this your home so quiet
        Live memories and ghosts of our time.
We are haunted by the feeling of a
        Roaring fireplace warming an ancient
Mead hall—
        Accented by love-worn books
And crevices holding secret treasures.

Fragrant Kaffe incenses the air.
        Soft glows burnishes the patina
Of blonde woods and polished pewter.
        Peace, security, warmth, comfort
Thrive in this dreamers' den of
        Music and books.

Timeless garret
        Scandinavian by design,
Poet's lair.

Heart's seed planted—sprouting,
        Not deflowered,
Just learning to bloom.

ELLEN TSAGARIS

LOVING YOU HAS EXHAUSTED ME

And so we come to this.
Polite stares and deafening
Silences.

Talked out with nothing more to
Say.

Passion and intimacy have now
Made us strangers.

We both dodge the past like
A bullet,
A bullet triggered by
A gun called memory.

Was it me, or you?
Was it important?
Who had the last word?

Who lost the scorecard?
Does it matter?

I'm so tired, bone tired,
Dead tired.

Loving you has exhausted me.
There simply is nothing left.

THE VAMPYRE DOLL COLLECTOR

She holds her first patient in her hand,
A limestone mother figure,
Her hair cornrowed, her face blank.

She daintily repairs a tiny break in
One long, sculpted row of braids,
Ancient dust lying on her old
Oak table in primeval miniature
Piles.

The full moon helps light her worktable.
The pale light of Hecate shines on the faces
Of her silent charges, lining the wall,
Silent witnesses to every historical epoch.

Here the stoic Ushabti mingles with the ancient Roman
Rag doll,
The delicate ivory fingers of a Bunraku
Puppet touch the satin robe of a Bartholomew Baby.

Tiny wooden daughters of Queen Anne rub
Microscopic shoulders with wax dolls dressed
In stiff gold lace,
Inhabitants of Baby Houses, once hers in long ago
Immortal childhood, themselves now 400 years gone.

Her milliners' models, her cornhusks and buckskin babies,
Gifts of the great chiefs of the great tribes,
The Sun Dolls, the Kachinas, the elegant
Lady brought to Roanoke by an Englishman and
Gifted her by a daughter of Powhatan,

The Nutcrackers and Mechanicals,
The Frozen Charlottes, the Noh masks
And African Fertility figures,

The Mlles. Huret, Thullier, Bru, Jumeau,
Mascotte, Eden, and Steiner,
Fräuleins Kestner, Simon, Halbig, Marseilles, Heubach, and the like,
All populate her shelves and nooks and crannies, where she works.

Heads and parts and bodies in this toy morgue reside
In jars and boxes,
Glass eyes peer from glass and crystal tubes once part
Of Dr. Frankenstein's lab,

Wracks of tiny dresses embroidered by Mary, Queen of Scots,
And Catherine, late of Aragon, and Nan Bullen, and Lady Jane,
All once her friends and confidantes,

SAPPHO, I SHOULD HAVE LISTENED

These line her cupboard shelves, and tin headed babies and
Metal young maidens take up space in her pantry where tinned beef
And canned soups were stored in more mundane households.

And all were her toys first; she had seen them new and shiny,
And their boxes and coffins, and trunks, where they had
Survived,
Lay hidden in her cellar and attic, carefully labeled
And preserved.

For millennia after millennia she had cared for them, her
Others,
Her Children, these "gentle vampires" crafted as icons
Of humanity,
Presents to her, the child that was made by a spirit,
That could not die,
That lived by night,

There were even a few dolls of the undead,
"Corpses" of living corpses,
Each holding a bit of herself, of her story,
Of her mother that she still remembered,
She who gave her that first doll,
The limestone Goddess she now
Cradled in the palm of her hand.

Each night for centuries she labored for them,
Each twilight she rose from her own doll-box,
Lightly dusting them with the feather duster
Given her by Queen Victoria's maid, along
With the little dolls loved by Dear Vicky herself.
Now these were her family, her human family long gone,
Her undead descendants scattered to the four corners,
More interested in feeding, and scaring, and dominating.

But she would go on, till time itself retired.
She would sit, and look forever
Young, she would Etsy and eBay and surf for more treasures,
She would curate, and organize, and subscribe to journals and
Make repairs, and sew impossibly tiny seams and
Restring limbs too delicate to survive, though they did,

And she, and her charges, would endure, seeking
Refuge in her immortal haven of Misfit dolls.

BALLET ENTRENOUS

Outside, we share a role amid this
>Burlesque of prodigies—

Celtic fringes in this farce where
>Would be Candides and Prima Donnas

Share top billing.
>We each perform a contradance—

As opposites and solo—
>But one day, in a cacophonous chorus—

We detect a simple harmony
>From there, we pas de deux into each other's arms.

I look into your eyes and follow your lead in
>This smoldering waltz of Eros,

Giselle to your Albrecht.
>You are the maestro, thrummer of my heart,

Transposer of my soul ..
>My body your score and instrument,

Awash, but not adrift, in your rhapsody of passion.
>Our bodies one Aeolian Harp,

The melody reaches it climax in our
>Harmony of ecstasy.

Choreographer of my trembling hands,
>Gentle guide of each pirouette as I dance a

Frenzied lover's ballet in your arms.
>You need my sweet agony with gossamer kiss

Blessed by Terpsichore.
>Echoes reverberate softly in

ELLEN TSAGARIS

Whispers lulled late in the dark.
    Ours is a masque of spent passions—
Two dancers drained for their art—
    Like a symphony of souls-or-lullaby of hearts.
Finally, the curtain of dreams falls—
    Our bodies entwined entrechat,
Pianissimo the hum of our breathing,
    As Morpheus takes the last bow.

FOR ANNE RICE

Deep before the time of
Akasha,
Before anyone could be damned,

Before Louis, and Lestat,
And Pandora, and
Claudia,

Earlier than even Maharet,
When there were no Mayfairs,
Or Lashers, and Blackwood
Farm was a marsh,

Before Damned Queens,
And East Edens, and
Beloved Belindas,

There was you,
And your typewriter,
And the stories in your
Heart's mind
Battling for freedom,

Fighting for room
With Sorrow, and Living,
And Family, and Texas.

ELLEN TSAGARIS

They fought on the
Sidewalks of Haight-Ashbury,
They crossed country to
Jackson Square and back.

They traipsed the globe,
And flew higher and faster
Than Marius,

But the epicure was you.
Your eyes saw what no one else could
You made a fantasy of history,

And an epic of fear.

Your rebel angels the more terrible
For there but for the Grace of God
Comes the Body Thief
For me.

SAPPHO, I SHOULD HAVE LISTENED

VAMPYRE

Victims, my victims? Or victims of ignorance and gloom?

Amnesty, for me none, family, friends, mother, father, gone

Mountains between freedom, and me, caverns wall me up

Pity, is there none? Promise of justice, of freedom? None?

Youth misspent, mine and others, games and frolics misunderstood

Revenge of old enemies, robbery and mayhem of my father's castle

Enigma, mystery, shrouds of truth, freedom, honor and justice

THE BLOOD COUNTESS
for Erzebet

"Justice, my lord,
Shall I have Justice?"

I say this to the barren
Wall, cold, stony, stoic.

Below more stones lie in wake,
Splotched with lichens, just lichens.

"Blood," cried all,
"Blood," swore my Cousin King,

"More Blood!" screamed the
Villagers—

Was it mine they wanted?
Was it mine they saw on the stones?

Was it maiden spilt, as I now
Stand judged of letting?

But where is my story?
When do lichens turn to Blood?

To Blood money for me?

Who speaks for me?
What ill fame cloaks me?

With no defense I am
Accused.

Blood, mine royal, damns me,
My trial is forbidden to me.

My husband is gone,
His blood spilled in battle.

For king and country he
Widowed me,

For greed and ransom,
He forfeited my home…

Blood of innocents is spilled,
Blood of ignorance

Blood of young girls I've never met,
Blood of crimes laid at my door

Till now, I stand and ask again
As the cold wind sighs through the cracks,

"Shall I have Justice,
Master Jailor?"

And the walls weep blood-red lichens
And reply, "For you never more."

DOPPELGÄNGER

Doppelgänger
    Double-glazed double-take
        Of woman

Soul-shackled in
    Perpetual adolescence
    Whored Madonna.

Violated ego—
    Vampired, fractured
    Frangible porcelain shattered.

Woman bisected into child
    Soul-torn automaton,
    Evil twin of herself.

Self-scissioned in tow—
    Parched dry husk
    Hag ridden.

Dim-sighted phantom
    Incorporeaous shroud
        Of a being.

Mirror shows
> A visual fallacy,
>> Schizoid image.

Viable woman
> Iced in glass,
> Dim reflection trapped.

Doppelgänger
> Breathes out life and
>> Sucks her soul.

LUCIFER; IF YOU COULD BE FORGIVEN

Child of the Morning Star,
Once beautiful and beloved,
Now fearsome and feared.
If you could be Forgiven,
Would you?

If you could be forgiven,
And given back your grace,
If you could be the Angel
With pure and blameless face?
Would you?

Would you love again your Maker?
Would you give Eve back her name?
Would you choose 'tween Cain and Abel?
Could you love mankind or sin?

CHIPPIANNOCK SANCTUARY

Alone in the hub of swarm
Heart shrouded in gossamer shadow,
Weary soul damned by sunlight
Harpy-hounded, soul devoured
By ivory bone.
No hiding place, no bandage for festering heart wounds
Lacerated with salt and gall
Sanity rent like rotted silk.

No hiding place but the corridors that lead to the dwellings
Of the Dead in this City of the Fallen.
Dulcet Death, seducer of
Desperate Hearts,
Of Captains of the River,
And Mothers with Babes in arms,
Of Brave Colonels
And Builders of Cities,

Purveyor of Peace, soothing shade
Soother for centuries,
Offer me the doss of Slumber deep
In this stone forest guarded by faithful
Limestone hounds
Where silent cradles rock and winds breathe through

Broken boughs.
Tranquil my mind, embalm my heart
Embrace my soul, close my eyelids with your cool touch.
Let a little stone lamb be my companion,
And remember me with a little stone bench.

There lies my grandmother's friend;
She cared for me like her own,
So that in part of our neighborhood,
I'm still Rose Marie's Little Girl.

There sleeps my sweet friend,
Double hearts marking her rest, but still
Not as big as the heart that beat within her
During life.

Across the hill sleeps another one dear,
Cut off the like cement trees on this or that
Ancient Grave.
He is with his grandfather, and our
Flowers mark our visits, growing more
And more Sorrow in our hearts.

Sweet Death, handmaid of
Chippiannock,
Listener of your citizens' tales,
Pilgrimage of those who would love your markers and
Your Stories,
Let your friendly worms enmesh me
To my Mother, Earth, and
Bind me to my father, Hades.
Dust the cool night with my Essence and let
A gentle pall
Silence my tortured soul.

A CHILD'S WINTER

Winter comes in the time of

Year

When bitter snows are

Quite, quite near

HYMN TO ARACHNE

Twisting, turning, taut and tense,

Weft and woof and

Hemp so dense,

Ikat colors

Hues hand-dyed

Stories told from

Days sublime.

Weaver's touch all

Magick conjure

Weave the colors

Patterns under

Cloak me now in

Wool and silk,

Woe to those

Who wish bad ilk.

ALLENSWORTH, CA

Allensworth was founded by three African Americans in 1908, and was the first town in California to be founded by African Americans. It survives today as a ghost town and State Park.

Chapped hands scooped up
Good earth.

They tilled the soil, things grew.
Houses, buildings, plants, trees,
People.

A little water made them all
Prosper under the hot desert sun.

Here, a tiny post office, portal
To the world,
Handed out stamps and letters,
The currency of communication.

There, a small school, taught
Small children dignity, and thrift,
And grace.

Then, one day, the water
Trickled out, and so did the people.

Spiders, snakes, scorpions
Trickled in,

Soon, the ghosts would be the
Storytellers.

ELLEN TSAGARIS

ON POE'S BICENTENNIAL

For my Mother, who walked through bad streets and dark alleys to find the home of Edgar Allan Poe one night when she was a graduate student

A solitary raven flew

Over my lonely door.

It was looking for my mother,

But would see her nevermore.

For the girl who walked out late

At night to find the poet's grave

With only an intrepid friend

To guide her lonely way,

Had grown, and moved, and gone to school.

Long after Edgar died.

She walked and walked that lonely

Night,

Young, vibrant, and alive.

No black cats crossed her happy

Path,

No pits and pendulums hung.

Ligia rested in her tomb,

And Ushers' house was one.

These many years that passed

Were often happy, but now they're gone.

And with them, now my mother's dust

Has mingled with poets' all.

DICKINSON MEETS HEMINGWAY

may be sung to the tune of "The Yellow Rose of Texas"

My life had stood a loaded gun
And so I shot the elk,
Then I said,
"Let's have a drink!"
And so I toast myself!"

SAPPHO, I SHOULD HAVE LISTENED

WITCH ETIQUETTE

"Double, Double, Toil and ..."
What?
Oh, alright, then,
Look up the next word in the
<u>Malleus.</u>
Trouble, Tarot, no Trouble, that's
It.
And, what's that aroma?
Eye of newt? Tongue of Toad?
Baby's breath?
Ah, an elixir - and it isn't even
Halloween.
"Shades of night and toe of bat,
Newborn baby stewed in vat" -
What? SHhh!!!!!!!
She's bidding Greymalkin
Conjure the Dragon -
No, I don't know which
Dragon, any more than I know
Which Witch.
Now you've done it!
I've warned you about those black
Cat and pointed hat jokes!

ELLEN TSAGARIS

She's lost her place,
She'll have to look it up in the
Index, "Toads, Tarot, Witch-Burning,
Ooops! wrong poem!"
"Sneer, if you like, but it says in my
<u>Shadow Book</u>, 'Woe to the sneerers -
They will grow bats' wings.'"
"We've burned our Holocaust - too -
I told the Dragon not to burn that king's a--,
What, Oh, alright, I'll start over."
"Double, double, toil and trouble -
burn that man, and on the double"
(p. 1313, *Malleus Mayhem, ch.5. How to Read your Tarot For Fun and Prophet.*)

ANNE AND SYLVIA

In Frenzy, you created, terrible sisters –
Rivals to the vapored end.
Sylvia's indictments burned,
Her quill wiped clean.
And Anne's stories dismissed as so much
Sound and Fury –
Misogyny reads madness for veracity and
Courage and vision.

And two prescient muses like gasping in the
Bell jar,
Withered fetuses of inspiration, whose
Only epitaph reads:
It's all the rage to be a dead lady poet.

HANGED WOMAN

How elegantly she swings in the breeze

That caresses wisps of flaxen

Hair and gossamer garments.

She dances with the wind, casting

Shadows against the obscene, glowering moon.

Slender, snapped neck, encased in a hempen necklace,

Her mouth opens in perpetual surprise.

Tongue expanding, a spectacular purple

Bloom budding between blue, leaf-like

Lips.

Eyes wide open to catch the world as her

Life flickers into eternity.

SAPPHO, I SHOULD HAVE LISTENED

Quoth the Muse,
"When some fool
Inspires Rage in your
Breast,
Sappho, stop that
Yapping tongue!"

O prescient one,
I should have listened,
Tattooed your wisdom on
My Heart.

For had I listened to your
Wisdom,
I'd now be free to
Ply my Art.

ACKNOWLEDGEMENTS

An earlier version of "Allensworth, CA" was published in *The Buffalo Soldier News Magazine*

"Chippiannock Sanctuary" was a featured poem in the 2010 Collins Poetry Residency

Jenson

The typeface used for this collection is Jenson. Nicolaus Jenson (1420-1480) is credited with creating the first roman typeface model. This version of Jenson is based upon his original roman archetype that inspired so many others.